Introduction

The structure of *Ginn History*

Ginn History is a programme of work that offers a clear and continuous approach for the whole of the primary age range. It offers practical advice and resources for all areas of National Curriculum history. To resource the core study unit 'Tudor and Stuart times', *Ginn History* provides the following resources:

At Key Stage 1

The Key Stage 1 *Ginn History* stories *Guy Fawkes* and *The Mayflower* will give children background knowledge of some of the personalities and events they will encounter in this study unit. The corresponding pictures in the Key Stage 1 *Group Discussion Book* will also introduce children to evidence from this period.

At Key Stage 2

The Key Stage 2 *Teachers' Handbook* provides complete support for the implementation of National Curriculum history, including guidance on curriculum planning, and full assessment and evaluation support. The *Teachers' Handbook* also contains guidance on how to teach the supplementary study units and how these units could be linked with 'Tudor and Stuart times'.

The *Tudor and Stuart times Pupils' Book* contains full coverage of National Curriculum content areas, specifically written with the attainment targets in mind.

The *Tudor and Stuart times Teachers' Resources* is designed to support the *Pupils' Book* by providing:
- Factual background information for each spread.
- Suggested activities for each spread to introduce and develop historical skills and understanding, and to link to other areas of the curriculum.
- Photocopiable *Blackline Master* activity sheets which help develop specific skills and act as a record for assessment.
- Three read-aloud stories which allow more in-depth focus on aspects of the period.
- Further references.

The *Pupils' Book*

The *Tudor and Stuart times Pupils' Book* introduces England in the 16th and 17th centuries. It focuses on the political changes and events in that period and on everyday life.

The materials in the book will prove useful for some of the supplementary units from list A of the National Curriculum programmes of study. For example:
- 'Ships and seafarers' would be enhanced by the inclusion of the Armada, pages 10/11; the *Mary Rose,* pages 32/33; Drake and Raleigh, pages 36-39; sea transport can be included via page 44.
- 'Houses and places of worship' relate to the sections on buildings and towns in Tudor and Stuart times on pages 24-29.
- 'Writing and printing' will benefit by including sections on Shakespeare from pages 34/35.
- 'Food and farming' can include a section on Tudor and Stuart farming from page 24.
- 'Land transport' will be extended by the use of page 30.
- 'Domestic life' can benefit from an inclusion of life in the country, pages 24/25, and life in the great houses, pages 26/27.

(More information on links between 'Tudor and Stuart times' and the supplementary units can be found in the Key Stage 2 *Teachers' Handbook*.)

Links with other programmes of study

It should also be pointed out that part of this period overlaps with the 'Exploration and Encounters' programme of study and so the two programmes of study could be merged to follow on one from another. 'Tudor and Stuart times' is a particularly difficult unit to deliver through general topic work. It may therefore be useful to combine 'Tudor and Stuart times' with 'Exploration and Encounters' in a history specific topic.

Attainment target links

Some attainment targets have been given in detail (e.g. **En 3/2d**) whilst others have been left more open (e.g. **Te 2**) because the nature of the activity means that children may respond at a variety of levels. Where **En 3** has been identified, teachers will also have the opportunity to assess **En 4** and **En 5** if they wish. **En 1** has not been identified at every discussion point.

TEACHERS RESOURCES

Contents

Introduction		3
The structure of Ginn History		3
The Pupils' Book		3
Links with other programmes of study		4
Attainment target links		4
***Pupils' Book* notes**		5
2/3	*The White Rose and the Red Rose*	5
4/5	*Henry VIII and his court*	5
6/7	*The break with Rome*	6
8/9	*Queen Elizabeth I*	6
10/11	*Armada*	7
12/13	*Roman Catholic plots*	8
14/15	*Charles I and the Civil War*	9
16/17	*The Second Civil War*	9
18/19	*Oliver Cromwell*	10
20/21	*Charles II*	10
22/23	*Tudor and Stuart family tree*	11
24/25	*Life in the country*	11
26/27	*Great houses*	12
28/29	*Life in the towns*	13
30/31	*Trade and travel*	13
32/33	*The loss of the Mary Rose*	14
34/35	*Shakespeare and the Globe*	15
36/37	*Adventurers – Sir Francis Drake*	15
38/39	*Adventurers – Sir Walter Raleigh*	15
40/41	*Plague*	16
42/43	*The Great Fire of London*	16
44/45	*Science*	17
46/47	*Religion and superstition*	18
Key *Tudor and Stuart* events		19
Further references		20
Read-aloud stories		21
The Royal prisoner (Charles I)		21
An Elizabethan merchant		24
The longest journey (Charles II)		26
Blackline Masters		29

Pupils' Book notes

2/3
The White Rose and the Red Rose

Background information

From 1450 onwards the two most powerful families in England, the House of York and the House of Lancaster, fought over the English crown. In 1483 the Yorkist king, Edward IV, died. He had two sons who were too young to rule so their uncle Richard ruled as regent. Richard III was crowned king in 1483. The two young princes, known as the 'Princes in the Tower', disappeared; many people believe that Richard had them killed.

In August 1485 the head of the Lancastrian family, Henry Tudor, raised an army. At Bosworth in Leicestershire Henry's army and Richard's army met. A third noble family headed by Lord Stanley also had an army present. Lord Stanley had not let it be known whose side he was on! As the battle progressed Richard's army began to win but suddenly Stanley's army charged in and Richard was killed and his army defeated. Richard III's crown was found in a bush and Henry was crowned.

Henry still had many problems, as the Yorkists tried to incite a number of rebellions. Henry wisely decided to marry the most important Yorkist, the daughter of Edward IV, Elizabeth. They had two sons and two daughters. In many ways Henry was a good king and he ruled very firmly. He established peace by keeping his barons under control, he gained a lot of money through taxation, he ruled through his council and courts and allowed Parliament to meet. When he died in 1509 his son had the backing of all of England's noble families.

Looking at evidence

Many of the stories about how unpleasant Richard III was were made in the early Tudor times. His portrait was altered to give him a hump on his back and he was accused of killing the Princes in the Tower. Much of this may have been Tudor propaganda.

Discussion and activities

- Ask the children whether they think Henry was a good king. **Hi 2/3**
- Discuss why some of the Tudors tried to make Richard seem a very unpleasant person. **Hi 2/2, 3/3**
- Henry taxed his barons and took some of their land. The barons wanted to keep soldiers to defend themselves. Who was right? **Hi 3/3**

4/5
Henry VIII and his court

Background information

Henry VIII

Henry came to rule a relatively peaceful England. He was actually Henry VII's second son but Arthur, the first, had died young. Thanks to his father's policies he had plenty of money and no real enemies. Life at court was a whirl of feasting, jousting, hunting and dancing at which Henry excelled. Henry was well educated, even to the point of being able to write in defence of Christianity for which the Pope gave him the title 'Defender of the Faith'. He was musical and even wrote his own compositions. His court was the centre of life for the noble families of England and received many embassies from abroad.

Catherine of Aragon

Aware of the troubles of the last century, Henry was very concerned that he should have a strong son to succeed him. Henry's first wife, Catherine of Aragon, was a Spanish princess who was previously married to Henry's brother Arthur. Catherine had several babies but only one, Mary, survived. Henry became desperate and told Cardinal Wolsey to ask the Pope to annul the marriage because it was against the laws of the Church (Catherine being his brother's widow). The Pope refused because he did not want to offend Catherine's nephew, the powerful Emperor Charles V. Thomas Cranmer, Archbishop of Canterbury granted Henry the divorce.

Anne Boleyn

Henry then married Anne Boleyn who gave birth to Elizabeth. Like Catherine she did not have a boy and Henry decided to remarry. He had Anne executed for unfaithfulness.

Jane Seymour

Jane Seymour was Henry's next wife. She gave birth to Edward but died a fortnight later. Edward was always a sickly child and died when he was just 15 years old.

Anne of Cleves

Henry then married Anne of Cleves. It was an arranged marriage, they had never seen each other and when they did, they did not like each other. The marriage was annulled almost immediately.

Catherine Howard

Catherine Howard was Henry's next wife. She was much younger than Henry. She was 19 and he was 49. Henry thought she was unfaithful with younger courtiers and therefore had her executed.

Catherine Parr

Henry's last wife was Catherine Parr. She had been married and widowed twice before. She took charge of his family and nursed him. She outlived Henry.

Looking at evidence

The Venitian ambassador described Henry VIII as 'so gifted and adorned with mental accomplishments of every sort that we believe him to have few equals in the world. He speaks English, French and Latin; understands Italian well; plays on almost every instrument; sings and composes fairly; is prudent and sage, and free from every vice.'

Discussion and activities

- Discuss why Henry was a popular king during his early years. **Hi 3/3**
- Discuss the way Henry treated his six wives. **Hi 3/3**
- Draw small portraits of Henry's wives and mount them in paper frames. **Ar**

6/7
The break with Rome

Background information

Protestantism

The 16th century was a period of religious change across Europe. Before 1500 almost all Christians in England acknowledged the Pope as the Head of the Roman Catholic Church. In Germany, Martin Luther had 'protested' about the Pope's power and the wealth of abbots and bishops. Many other people shared the desire to return to a simpler church like the early church, so various Protestant Churches were founded.

Wolsey

Cardinal Wolsey is probably best remembered for building Hampton Court Palace. He was Henry's chief adviser but could not organise the annulment of Henry's marriage to Catherine of Aragon, and so was dismissed.

The Church of England

When the Pope would not give Henry an annulment of his marriage to Catherine of Aragon, Henry got his own Archbishop to arrange the divorce for him. Henry wanted to break the power of the Pope in England and to do so, he got his Parliament to pass the Act of Supremacy. This made Henry the Head of the Church of England. Henry was not a Protestant but when he died his son's councillors were. Once he had broken with Rome, Henry realised that he could take many of the riches of the Church. In many monasteries Henry was not recognised as the Head of the Church. By passing the Dissolution of the Monasteries Bill in 1536, Parliament closed down all the monasteries and gave Henry all the wealth to use as he saw fit.

Discussion and activities

- Why did Henry dissolve the monasteries? What do the children think Tudor people would have thought about the Dissolution of the Monasteries? Would it have depended on whether they were a monk, an abbot, a noble given more land, or a farmer paying taxes to the monastery? The children could each adopt the role of a Tudor person, and debate this issue. **Hi 1/3b, 2/2, 3/3**
- BLM 1 – Looking at the reasons why Henry dissolved the monastries. **Hi 1/3b**

8/9
Queen Elizabeth I

Background information

Edward VI

When Henry VIII died in 1547 the Protestant religion made rapid gains. Against a background of inflation and economic uncertainty, England was ruled by Edward's advisers. When they were not intriguing against each other they were busy tightening the Protestant hold on the country.

Lady Jane Grey

Edward was always sickly and died in 1553. His chief adviser, the Lord Protector, John Dudley Duke of Northumberland tried to keep his power by making his own daughter-in-law, Lady Jane Grey, Queen. Support for Northumberland collapsed and Henry VIII's second child, Mary, became Queen. Lady Jane Grey is remembered as the nine day queen. She was executed with her husband.

Queen Mary

As the daughter of Catherine of Aragon, Mary was a devout Catholic. The Protestants who did not flee abroad were persecuted. About 300 people were burned within the first three years of Mary's reign.

Mary became known as 'Bloody Mary' and was unpopular with her subjects. Mary had married the Catholic King of Spain, Philip, and her alliance with Spain was also unpopular. It was during Mary's reign that the last bit of continental Europe was lost to England. The port of Calais had been in England's hands for centuries. When Mary died in 1558 her younger sister became Queen.

Queen Elizabeth I

Elizabeth had always had to be careful when Mary was Queen and had lived a life constantly under suspicion, as she would have been an ideal figurehead for a plot against Mary. At one time Elizabeth was imprisoned in the Tower of London. She became Queen in 1558 when she was 25. Elizabeth succeeded to the throne of a fairly poor, weak country by European standards. England's position certainly changed under her long reign. Elizabeth had been well-educated. One of her tutors was Roger Ascham, a famous scholar of the time.

Elizabeth had a great many fashionable clothes, and naturally she set the fashion in England. She kept lists of all her gifts and possessions. When she died she is said to have owned 3,000 dresses. Many of the fabrics were brought from Italy or France and were very expensive. In 1560 she was given a New Year's present by one of her courtiers of the first pair of silk stockings in England.

It was important for the monarch to be seen so Elizabeth, like most of her predecessors, often moved around the southern part of England. Her main palace was Whitehall; others included St James Palace, Somerset House, Durham House, Richmond Palace, Hampton Court Palace and Nonesuch Palace. When Elizabeth moved so did much of her furniture and her servants and all the courtiers. The procession must have been an amazing sight, unless it was coming to your house, and then the thought of the expense of keeping Elizabeth and her court must have been quite daunting!

Suitors

Elizabeth remained unmarried for her whole life. It is thought that Robert Dudley, Earl of Leicester and the French Duc d'Alencon were her most famous suitors. Elizabeth herself proclaimed that she was married to her country. The quotation in the cartoon (on page 9) comes from Camden's History written in 1586.

Looking at evidence

This is what Roger Ascham wrote about Elizabeth:
'She has just passed her sixteenth birthday and shows such dignity and gentleness as are wonderful at her age. She talks French and Italian as well as she does English and has often talked to me readily and well in Latin, moderately in Greek. When she writes Greek and Latin nothing is more beautiful than her handwriting. She delights as much in music as she is skilful in it.'

When Elizabeth visited Lord North for three days he had to provide all of the following foods: 67 sheep; 34 pigs; 4 stags and 16 bucks used for 176 pasties; 1,200 chickens; 363 capons; 33 geese; 6 turkeys; 237 dozen pigeons; a great many pheasants and partridges; cartloads of oysters and fish; 2,500 eggs and 430lbs of butter.

Discussion and activities

- Read Roger Ascham's report about Elizabeth to the children. How does her education compare with theirs? **Hi 1/2c, 3a, 3/3**
- **BLM 4** – Elizabeth was particularly fond of miniature paintings. Draw a miniature of an Elizabethan person. **Ar**
- Using a computer package such as Front Page Xtra get the children to write an account of Elizabeth on procession. **Te 5/3a; En 3**
- **BLM 2** – Making a programme of events to amuse Elizabeth. **En 3/2d**
- **BLM 3** – Looking at evidence written about Elizabeth I. **Hi 2/6**

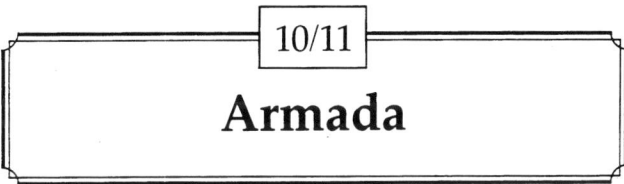

10/11 Armada

Background information

The Armada was not a sudden occurrence. Europe was divided into Protestant and Catholic states who sided against each other over most issues. Elizabeth had been at war with Spain since her intervention in the Netherlands (Protestant) attempt to gain independence from Spain (Catholic). As early as 1568 Elizabeth had confiscated a large amount of silver that was bound from Spain to the Netherlands as payment for the Spanish army. The Spanish monarch, Philip, was often near bankruptcy but fortunately Spain had the reserves of gold and silver they had stolen from the Americas. English seamen like Hawkins and Drake were not allowed to trade in the 'New World' and so often stole Spanish gold. The Spaniards called this piracy. In 1585 Elizabeth sent an army to the Netherlands under the command of the Earl of Leicester. Philip ordered the seizure of all English shipping, so Elizabeth sent Drake to loot Spanish trading posts, towns and ships for gold.

Armada in preparation

In 1586 Philip began to prepare a huge fleet. Drake daringly raided Cadiz in the spring of 1587, and burnt 24 ships and their supplies. This put the Armada back a year and gave England more time to prepare. The fleet was prepared and across the country fires were built on high ground to act as warning beacons should the Spaniards land.

Armada in action

The Armada consisted of 130 ships carrying 20,000 soldiers. The Spaniards were not trying to defeat the English at sea; they knew that Hawkins had built up a good navy and that the English ships were more manoeuvrable. Instead they planned to use the Armada as a means of transferring soldiers from the Netherlands to England. As it sailed up the English Channel the Armada was harassed by the English fleet. The fireships' attack at Calais and the Battle of Gravelines effectively destroyed the will of the Spaniards and many of their ships. They fled north and were battered by storms that finished off the great Armada.

Looking at evidence

An eyewitness described the ships in the Armada as follows:

'The speediest vessels in that Armada . . . seemed in comparison (with English ships) to be standing still'.

The eyewitness said the English ships 'could nimbly come and go and fetch the wind with the best advantage'.

Medina Sidonia, a Spanish naval commander, described the attack at Calais:

'Suddenly eight ships with sail set, and driven with wind and tide, came straight towards us, all burning fiercely. Fearing they might contain explosion machines, I gave the order to weigh anchor. When the fire-ships had passed by, I meant to return to the same position. My flagship and some other ships near her did anchor. But the current was so strong that it swept the rest of the Armada far away. They did not see us, and were driven off as far as Dunkirk'.

Discussion and activities

- Using a local map of 1:50000 or 1:25000 scale see if the children can identify any local Beacon Hills; the children can give the four figure coordinates so that others can locate them. Use an atlas to identify Spain, the Netherlands, Calais, and Cadiz. **Gg 1/4a, 4e**
- Look at the 16th century painting of the defeat of the Armada (page 11), and then get the children to do their own drawings depicting the scenes of the Armada. **Ar**
- Draw the story of the Armada in cartoon form. Add text underneath. The text must explain why the Armada came. **Ar; En 3; Hi 1/3b**
- Write newspaper articles about the Armada from either the Spanish or the English point of view. **En 3; Hi 2**
- Compare Tudor warships with warships of another time, e.g. Roman, Viking or Greek warships. **Hi 1/3c**
- Ask the children to make a model in a box (diorama) to show what life on board ship was like. **Te**
- BLM 5 – Putting the events of the Armada in chronological order. **Hi 1/1a**
- BLM 6 – Plotting the course of the Spanish Armada. **Gg**

12/13 Roman Catholic plots

Background information

Mary Queen of Scots

As a result of a civil war in Scotland, Mary Queen of Scots fled to England. Mary was replaced by her Protestant son, James VI. This put Elizabeth in a difficult position. She could hardly hand Mary, a fellow monarch, back to her rebellious subjects. Nor could she make war on the Protestant Scots to reinstate the Catholic Mary. Having Mary in England though gave a focus of attention for the Catholics who wanted to overthrow Elizabeth. Mary was kept in close confinement but still was the focus of plots. In 1586 Babington's plot led Elizabeth to agree reluctantly to Mary's execution. She was executed at Fotheringay Castle on 8th February 1587.

James I

When Elizabeth died in 1603 few of her subjects could remember a time when she had not been Queen. Many were worried because Elizabeth had no children to succeed her and would not name her successor. Her councillors had worked to ensure the smooth transfer of power to James VI of Scotland, who became James I of England. As a Scot, James was seen as a foreigner. Many English people found his speech difficult to follow and he took a while to understand the way England was ruled. James was a Protestant but was inclined to be lenient to the Catholics. Parliament was strongly Protestant (Puritan) and persuaded James to be tough with the Catholics.

The Gunpowder plot

In response to the political situation, a conspiracy was formed to blow up the Houses of Parliament when James was due to open them. Guy Fawkes was an expert in the use of gunpowder and returned from the Netherlands to help. The conspirators rented a house next to the House of Lords and a storage room under the Lords. The plot was brought to the attention of the King's chief minister, Robert Cecil, because of the letter to Mounteagle. Thus Cecil ensured that Parliament was well guarded. Some historians have wondered whether Robert Cecil might not have been behind the plot so as to have an excuse for dealing harshly with Catholics. The failure of the plot stopped Catholics from plotting against the King. It further increased the suspicion and hatred between Catholics and Protestants.

Discussion and activities

- Read the *Ginn History Guy Fawkes* story to the class (page 88 in the *Key Stage One Teachers' Resource Book*).
- Discuss Robert Cecil's role. Did he help make up the plot to frighten Catholics? If so, why did he? **Hi 1/3b, 2**
- Ask the children to discuss why the conspirators wanted to kill James. What did they hope to gain? **Hi 1/3b**
- At his trial, Guy Fawkes said, 'I am sorry for nothing but that the act was not performed'. Discuss with the children what this quotation tells us about Guy Fawkes' character. **Hi 3/3**
- BLM 7 – Writing Guy Fawkes' confession. **Hi 1/3b**

14/15

Charles I and the Civil War

Background information

Charles I

When James died his son Charles became king. Charles was a short man with a stutter and he did not have the political skills of his father. In the first four years of his reign the country became involved in wars with France and Spain. Charles found it impossible to obtain funds from Parliament and eventually, having made peace, Charles decided to rule without Parliament. For 11 years Charles ruled successfully without a Parliament but he made a fatal error when he tried to spread the way the Church of England worshipped into Scotland. The Scots rose in revolt and marched into England. Charles had to call a Parliament to get enough money to raise an army to fight the Scots. So in 1640 what became known as the 'Long Parliament' sat for the first time.

The road to war

Parliament was not willing to give Charles money unless he met some of their demands. As some of his old trusted advisers were executed or exiled the gap between Charles and Parliament grew bigger so that by 1642 both sides were almost ready for war. Charles tried to arrest five Members of Parliament, including John Pym, by taking soldiers into Parliament. He failed and fled to York to collect an army. People all over the country were divided – should they support Charles or Parliament?

The first Civil War

After a number of successes, it seemed that Charles might win. Then Parliament got Oliver Cromwell to reform its army; they became better trained, were paid more regularly and given better equipment. This New Model Army eventually defeated Charles' forces with the help of the Scots at the Battle of Marston Moor. The remaining Royalists were defeated at Naseby but Charles escaped.

The musketeers

The soldiers on both sides were very similar to begin with. Often it was only a battle cry or a token such as heather stuck in a headband that indicated who was on which side.

Musketeers carried matchlock muskets which, at that time, were slow single shot guns that were so heavy that they were often used with a rest. They were fired by touching a lit cord to a small amount of gunpowder. Often they did not work at all in the damp.

Some musketeers wore their everyday clothes; others might have a buff leather jacket to help protect them. Over their shoulders they wore a belt with a dozen or so wooden bottles each carrying enough powder to charge the musket. There would also be a bag of bullets and a powder flask on this belt. Musketeers had to be protected from cavalry by pikemen.

The pikemen

Pikemen had to be strong to manage a 16 to 18 foot pike. Usually they wore an iron helmet and some iron body armour. They also carried swords that they would use if their pikes broke.

The cavalry

The cavalry were the elite of the soldiers; many were noblemen and were well-equipped. Many had expensive clothing that they liked to wear. They would all have buff leather coats and most wore iron breastplates.

They fought with two pistols and swords, firing the pistols just as they charged in.

Gradually the Parliamentarians got better equipment: their new muskets were quicker to load and more reliable. To begin with the Cavaliers were better cavalrymen but gradually the Parliamentarians became more disciplined. As they became successful so Parliament's army became bigger than the King's.

Discussion and activities

- Using a map of your county or of Great Britain, look for Civil War battlefields. Locate them using four figure references. **Gg 1/4a**
- Make pictures to show the similarities and differences between the two armies. Compare the soldiers with soldiers from another time, e.g. Roman legionaries. **Hi 1/3c, 4a**
- Let the children write a pamphlet in support of either the King or Parliament. **En 3**
- BLM 8 – Looking at the points of view of cavaliers and roundheads. **Hi 2**

16/17

The Second Civil War

Background information

The second war

From 1645 to 1649 the situation in England was very confused. Charles had been defeated but many people still considered him King. He made many agreements but refused to keep them. The Scots felt they had a right to have a say in what happened in England and Charles was nearly able to use this to his advantage. Eventually Charles persuaded the Scots to invade England to restore him to the throne but the army was defeated and this sealed Charles' fate. He escaped to Carisbrooke Castle on the Isle of Wight, where he became a prisoner. It became obvious that he could not be allowed to remain as a focus of discontent. The Parliamentarian force was in danger of splitting into many different factions.

Charles' trial and execution

Eventually Parliament decided to try Charles for treason. In fact they did so on a day when Colonel Pride took some musketeers in to Parliament to exclude those who might have wanted to support the King. Charles was brought to the Palace of Westminster before a court of MPs. Charles refused to recognise the right of the court to try him; keeping his hat on was symbolic of this. Eventually he was found guilty and condemned to death as a tyrant, traitor and public enemy. The death warrant was signed by his enemies. (Charles II was later to punish the surviving regicides). The King was executed on 30th January 1649. The student (Philip Henry) whose eyewitness account is given in part (in the cartoon on page 17) makes clear that many people were rather afraid of what had been done.

Discussion and activities

- Ask the children what they would have done with Charles I. Would they have killed him or left him to live out his life in prison? Ask the children what they think it would have been like to be part of the crowd at Charles' execution.
- Read the story 'The Royal prisoner' on page 21. Do the children think Henry Firebrace was right to help Charles escape? **Hi 2**
- If the children had been Charles, would they have fled abroad; tried to fight on with Scottish help; or agreed to live quietly in a country house? Try to get them to justify their decision. **Hi 3/3**
- Re-enact the trial of Charles I. This time Charles should speak up for himself. Who else might speak up for him? Was he really a tyrant, traitor and public enemy? What reasons can the prosecution give for having him found guilty? **Hi 1/3b, 4b; En1**
- BLM 9 – Writing a newspaper report about the execution of Charles I. **En 3/2b**

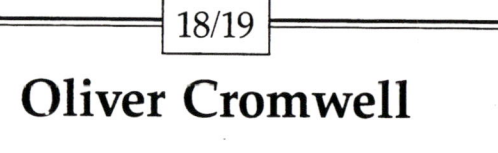

18/19
Oliver Cromwell

Background information

Cromwell

Oliver Cromwell was a landowner who had been brought up near Huntingdon and farmed near Ely. He was elected to the Long Parliament and spoke out against the King. Cromwell was one of the major forces behind the creation of the New Model Army and this gave him his power base.

The Interregnum (1649-1660)

For 11 years Britain was ruled as a republic. Using the power of the New Model Army, Cromwell subdued both the Scots and the Irish. For the first time the three countries were ruled by the same administration. Abroad, the Dutch were defeated between 1652-54, parts of the Caribbean were captured from the Spaniards and in 1658 they were defeated in a land battle near Dunkirk.

The Lord Protector

Much of this success was as a result of the personal rule of Cromwell. After the death of Charles I the Long Parliament ruled but there was so much chaos and indecision that eventually Oliver Cromwell closed Parliament and took the title of Lord Protector. Cromwell summoned two parliaments, and quarrelled with them both. When Oliver Cromwell died in 1658 his son Richard temporarily stepped into his shoes, but chaos quickly ensued and the nation turned back to the monarchy.

Puritan England

Puritans were an extreme group of Protestants. Cromwell was a Puritan, and during his rule many puritanical laws were passed to govern everyday life. Many of these were not at all popular with the mass of people.

Charles II evades capture

In 1651 Cromwell defeated a Scots and English Royalist army at Worcester. Charles II had to flee from this defeat. This flight included his hiding in an oak tree, possibly in Staffordshire. He wore many disguises, including that of a servant. He eventually escaped to France.

Discussion and activities

- Try to obtain booklets about Hinchingbrooke House in Cambridgeshire to find out about Cromwell's home.
- Discuss with the children whether they think the Interregnum was a success. Ask them to make a list of reasons for and against the Interregnum. **Hi 1/3b, 3/3**
- The Cromwell Museum, Huntingdon, holds many artefacts connected with Oliver Cromwell's life.

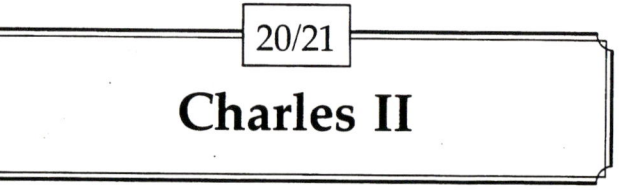

20/21
Charles II

Background information

Charles II

After his escape from England in 1651 Charles II remained on friendly terms with the English Royalists. Following the chaos of Cromwell's rule Charles was invited to return to England to be King. He came ashore at Dover on 25th May 1660. Charles was very popular at first. He forgave most of his father's enemies, except those who had signed the death warrant, and was determined to enjoy himself.

He summoned Parliament and restored the Church of England in place of the more puritanical Church of the Interregnum.

Things soon started to go wrong for Charles. He never had enough money and fought two short but unsuccessful wars against the Dutch. On one occasion the Dutch fleet actually sailed up the Thames.

Charles died in 1685 leaving no children and was succeeded by James II, his brother.

James II

James was a Catholic and gradually introduced a number of measures to bring back Catholicism. People were prepared to put up with that until the birth of his son in 1688 foreshadowed a long line of Catholic rulers. James was replaced by his daughter, Mary, and her Protestant husband, William of Orange. It is from their reign that the idea of the supremacy of Parliament really became practice.

Pepys

Pepys' diary provides the best source about the Stuarts during the Restoration. There are graphic accounts of the Fire, the Plague, the Dutch wars, as well as a whole lot of incidentals about daily life. Pepys wrote in a form of shorthand so his diaries need transcribing for school use. He was born in London in 1633, the son of a tailor. He won a scholarship to go to Cambridge University and went on to work in the Admiralty. He soon rose to become the Secretary to the Navy Board.

Looking at evidence

Another famous diarist of the period was John Evelyn. This is what he wrote about the Restoration:
'With a triumph of above 2,000 horse and foot, brandishing their swords and shouting with irrepressible joy; the ways strewed with flowers, the bells ringing, the streets hung with tapestry, the fountains running with wine ... I stood in the Strand and blessed God ... All this was done without one drop of blood shed, and by that very army which rebelled against him.'

Discussion and activities

- Discuss with the children why people were pleased to have the King back. Who would be pleased to see him restored and who might not be so pleased? **Hi 2**
- The children could write diaries of the week. Alternatively they could write a diary for a real or imaginary person in history. This would be a good follow on from Pepys. Paper can be 'aged' with cold tea. **En 3**
- Discuss with the children the question 'Who rules the country today?'
- Read the extract from John Evelyn and then ask the children to write a small passage about the King's return. Encourage the children to think about whether they would actually welcome the return of the King. **Hi 1/3b, 3/3**

- BLM 11 – Designing a 'wanted' poster for Charles II. **En 3/2d**
- BLM 10 – Writing about the points of view of the crowd at the coronation of Charles II. **Hi 2**
- Read the story 'The longest journey' on page 26. Ask the children to present the story in drama or cartoon form after listening to the story. **Hi 3**

22/23
Tudor and Stuart family tree

Background information

The family tree shows the Tudor family tree from Henry VII to Elizabeth I, the link through Henry's daughter Margaret to the Stuarts, and the link from James II to the last of the Stuart monarchs, William and Mary and then Anne.

Discussion and activities

- Construct a family tree for the present Royal Family. Use pictures cut from newspapers and magazines to illustrate each of the members of the family.
- Either individually, or in groups, depict the childrens' families as generation charts or family trees. (See page 17 of the *Key Stage One Teachers' Resource book*.)

24/25
Life in the country

Background information

The farming village

The majority of people lived and worked in the country. Over much of the country the 'open field system' survived. The cultivated land of the village was divided into three large fields which were sown with cereals or left fallow. Each villager was given a number of strips which he worked and harvested himself. By the 16th century things were changing, especially in the south of England. Clever and wealthier landlords bought up their neighbours' strips and began to put hedges around their new fields, or enclosures as they were called. The use of enclosures meant that gradually some farmers (yeomen) became more wealthy than the average villager. The gentry (squires or lords of the manor) were still the most important group. The ordinary villager might be worse off than his ancestors as he lost land.

PUPILS' BOOK NOTES   11

Women might work as dairymaids or midwives or might spin and weave wool at home. Otherwise there was plenty to do at home: animals to tend, garden to cultivate, children to feed and clothe, as well as seasonal work in the fields. Men would work the whole year round with the exception of the holy days and Sundays.

Food

The harvest set the quality and quantity of food. Rye bread, supplemented by cheese and washed down by ale or beer, was the staple diet. As the two centuries passed, fresh vegetables and fruit were grown in small gardens, and meat, poultry and fish might be afforded on special days. Food was cooked in a cauldron or spit over the fire. Only a knife was used as cutlery, and drinks were taken from horn beakers.

Houses

Houses in the country were made from a timber frame that had branches woven together (wattle) in between the timber. The wattle was then made weather proof by being covered with daub: various mixtures of mud, clay, straw and dung. Furniture was likely to consist of just the essentials: a trestle table, a bench, stools, a spit or cauldron over a hearth and straw mattresses as beds. Wealthier farmers had larger houses and might also have an oak table, four-poster bed, an oak armchair, a chest and a wooden cradle. Glass was rarely used except by the very wealthy so there would be small windows with shutters.

The church

The parson was one of the few people able to read and write and the Bible in the church might be the only book in the village. Most people had to stand in the church; only the rich sat in pews.

Leisure

How much leisure time you had depended on how wealthy you were. Activities like hunting were very popular among the wealthy. Morris dancing, wrestling, football, bowls, and cockfighting were popular pastimes. May Day was the best day of celebration with dancing around the maypole. The level of violence in games such as football is described by Philip Stubbs in the cartoon on page 25. He wrote this in 1583.

Discussion and activities

- Ask the children to use the photograph on page 24 as a source of evidence for a series of cartoons depicting life in the country. **Hi 1/4c**
- Discuss with the children which items of furniture would be considered essential by a Tudor villager. Ask them to decide how that differs from today's essentials. **Hi 1/3a**

- Timber framed houses can be made using balsa wood as the frame, or simply by painting a box to represent the framework. **Te**
- Have a Tudor style May Day celebration. Try making a maypole and getting the children to make up a dance.

26/27
Great houses

Background information

The houses

Traditionally houses were built of wood but the increasing use of wood for making charcoal meant that houses were being built of brick. The Great Hall was used for dining and entertaining and the wings for bedrooms. Towards the end of the period the newest style had a smaller hall and separate dining and entertaining rooms. Rooms were decorated with plaster ceilings, panelled wood walls and marble and alabaster additions. Decoration was a sign of wealth. Glass was available in small pieces for windows and so was set in lead (leaded lights) to make large windows. Some houses were raised up on a basement that could then be used for the kitchens. Furniture was made from wood and elaborately carved. Grinling Gibbons was a master wood carver.

Gardens and parks

Big houses were surrounded by gardens and parks. Formal gardens were made using bow hedges and flowers. Mazes were planted to amuse visitors. Surrounding the gardens would be parks for hunting deer and hare, for falconry, or firework displays.

Looking at evidence

The following quotation refers to the self-sufficiency of the Verney household who lived at Claydon House in Buckinghamshire:
'A great house provisioned itself with little help. The inhabitants brewed and baked, they churned and ground their meal, they bred up, fed and slew their beeves (cattle – hence 'beef') and sheep, and brought up their pigeons and poultry at their own doors. Their horses were shod at home, their planks were sawn, their rough ironwork was forged and mended . . .'

Discussion and activities

- A visit to a local great house would be interesting, but be aware that many have had later additions. This could then be the stimulus for a display including models of houses, the children's own mazes, the furniture of the time, etc. **Hi 1/3c, 3/3**

- Ask the children to work on a dance drama. Some of them should represent servants, others visitors, and still others the owners.

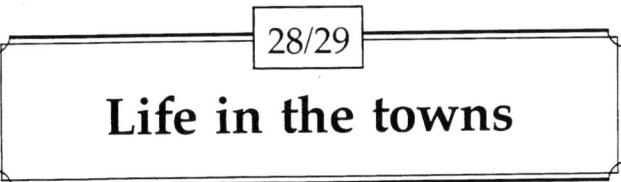
Life in the towns

Background information

Town houses

Most houses in the town were similar to small country houses. Gradually they were replaced by timber framed houses of two or three storeys. To provide more space upstairs these upper storeys often projected over the lower storeys. This made the streets very dark and crowded. These houses might have chimneys, a tiled or thatched roof and windows with glass in them. Most merchants and craftsmen lived and worked in the same building, the shop part of the building being open to the street. Towns also had many inns, a market hall, a grammar school and a guildhall. Some of these more important buildings would be built of stone.

Apprentices

The craftspeople had a careful system for training apprentices. They would have to be indentured to the craftspeople for seven years during which time they would gradually learn their craft until they could be considered a journeyman. Apprentices were easily recognised in the streets as they wore blue uniforms. They were often blamed for unruly behaviour. Journeymen could only become master craftsmen by recognition from the guild.

Guilds

The guild was a way for groups of craftspeople or merchants to collect together to protect themselves. Prices could be fixed and quality maintained. The guild would meet at the guildhall and it was there that customers could complain if treated unfairly.

The streets

Streets were fairly unpleasant in the Tudor and Stuart period. They were narrow, dark, and full of rubbish. The habit of householders emptying chamber pots into the streets from upstairs windows could not have helped, especially if you hadn't heard the warning cry of 'regardez vous'.

Many streets were named after the craft or trade that was practised in them, e.g. Butcher Row.

Law and order

The towns were run by the wealthy craftspeople and merchants. They elected a mayor to act as their figurehead. Poor people had no say in the way the town was run.

London

London was the largest town though even then you could walk from Charing Cross to the country. Gradually the business of government centred on Westminster and many important people from around the country and from abroad lived in London so as to be near the seat of government. The River Thames was an important route for travel in the town. It also froze over several times in the Stuart period to provide a wonderful ice rink. London Bridge was still the only bridge over the river in the London area. Its narrow roadway was lined with houses, each with a ground floor shop.

Discussion and activities

- Make models of houses and shops from boxes and produce a street scene. A frieze could be made accompanied by written work about town life. **Hi 1/4c**
- Children should discuss or list the improvements that have been made to town life since Tudor and Stuart times. **Hi 1/3a, 3b**
- Discuss with the children whether they would prefer to live in the town or the country in the 16th century. Ask them to look carefully at the evidence. **Hi 3/3**
- BLM 12 – Designing a Tudor shop sign. **Ar**
- Read the story 'An Elizabethan merchant' on page 24 to the children.

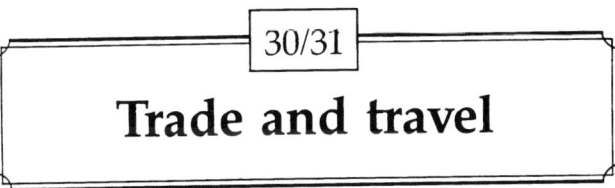
Trade and travel

Background information

Coinage and trade

The exchanging of goods was still the simplest form of commerce. Gradually as markets widened the use of money or tokens became greater. The advantage of coinage was that it was worth the same throughout the realm. Coins also provided a handy way of reminding the people who was king or queen. Remember that 12 pennies made a shilling and 20 shillings a pound. The main export from England throughout the period was wool. In Tudor times it was almost the only export.

Roads

The major land routes were based on the Roman roads. These were built as straight and direct as possible, often using causeways over boggy ground and bridging rivers. They were difficult to keep in good repair in a land where there was no central system. Each parish or town was responsible for the upkeep of its roads and despite many laws some didn't do a good job. Some of the wealthier classes preferred to go by carriage during the Stuart period. Then some roads were taken over by private companies who charged tolls to keep them in repair. Even on these 'turnpike' roads travel was still uncomfortable and could be dangerous. Following the Civil War there was an increase in the number of highwaymen.

In towns, richer people could afford to hire a hackney carriage or even a sedan chair.

Water

Some loads were just too heavy or too fragile to move by land and so the rivers and coastal waters were an important trade route.

Sea

Commerce and communications with Europe had grown. Packet ships were ideal for cross-Channel trade, carrying wool or fish from England and returning with wine and timber. During Tudor and Stuart times richer merchants and adventurers began to take bigger ships across the oceans. Their ships sailed from London, Bristol and Liverpool to Africa and the Americas. A very profitable trade was the taking of slaves from Africa to the Americas. The most famous trading posts became those in the Americas but many were established on the west coast of Africa as well.

Discussion and activities

- **BLM 14** – Looking at different points of view about the road system. **Hi 2/5**
- The children could assume the role of a Tudor or Stuart person. Discuss what they think about the road system. Do we really know or are we just guessing? **Hi 2/4**
- Children should make a frieze showing the different forms of transport during Tudor and Stuart times. **Hi 1/4c**
- Compare the Tudor and Stuart road system with the system that we have today. In what ways are the methods of transport better or worse, similar or different? **Hi 1/3a**

32/33
The loss of the *Mary Rose*

Background information

Mary Rose

King Alfred was the first monarch to stress the importance of having a well-equipped modern navy. The *Mary Rose* was one of the most up-to-date ships of the Tudor time, having been newly built in 1510.

The Mary Rose sinks

On Sunday 19th July 1545 Henry VIII watched the *Mary Rose* leave Portsmouth harbour. Suddenly and without warning she heeled over and sank in under a minute. Fortunately she settled into thick mud which preserved much of the ship. No one knows exactly why the ship sank. The French even claimed to have been responsible as she was engaged in a sea battle. Most experts now believe that she was top heavy, carrying too many soldiers and too many cannons, and had the portholes open for firing.

The raising of the Mary Rose

Ever since she sank efforts have been made to raise the *Mary Rose*. In 1982 a team of archaeologists and divers led by Margaret Rule and aided by considerable heavy lifting equipment managed to refloat her and take her to Portsmouth where she can now be seen.

Looking at evidence

Thanks to the speed with which she sank and the thick mud in which she settled the Mary Rose gives a good picture of life aboard a Tudor warship. A whole range of items have been found (some of which are pictured on page 33):
- Leather shoes and slippers, leather jerkins, hose and tunics;
- Long bows and arrows for the soldiers to shoot from the rigging at the enemy;
- Large cannons, one made of iron and bound with iron hoops to strengthen the barrel, another cast from bronze;
- Cooking and eating equipment such as cauldrons, wooden bowls, and pewter plates and spoons, bottles and wine flagons;
- The remains of food such as peapods, nut shells, plum and cherry stones, fish bones and animal bones including cattle, sheep, deer, pigs and poultry;
- Tools and navigational aids such as portable sundials, a magnetic compass, a carpenter's plane, an iron nail, tar, ropes, blocks and pulleys;
- Means of entertainment such as musical instruments, dice, backgammon and chess;
- The barber-surgeon's tools including razors, a saw for amputating limbs, a heavy mallet, a mortar and pestle and a blood letting bowl;

Discussion and activities

- Ask the children to make their own drawings of life at sea based on the evidence on these pages and pages 36-39 on Drake and Raleigh. **Hi 3/2**
- Blocks and tackle were used by Tudor seamen to lift heavy loads. What devices can the children plan and make to lift a heavy load? **Te**
- Write an entry for a sailor's diary. Include information about what sailors they ate on board, and how they spent their leisure time. How much of this information can be backed up by evidence?

34/35
Shakespeare and the Globe

Background information

Shakespeare

Shakespeare came from a large family; he had six brothers and sisters. Shakespeare probably started his theatrical career as a stage hand. He joined the company of Richard Burbage, a famous actor of the time, called the Lord Chamberlain's Company. Most actors of this time were looked down on as some sort of vagabond. However, the Lord Chamberlain's Company was invited to perform in front of Queen Elizabeth. James I also liked plays and requested that the company be renamed the King's Men. Shakespeare became quite a wealthy man with a share in the Globe Theatre and the Blackfriars Theatre.

The Globe

During the last part of Elizabeth's reign, theatre became popular entertainment. Strolling players went around the towns and acted in the courtyards of inns which were open to the sky. The Globe was opened in Shoreditch in East London but Burbage moved it in 1599 to Southwark. Plays were an entertainment that appealed to and catered for all classes, from the groundlings who might pay a penny to stand on the floor to the wealthier who could buy gallery seats or even sit on the stage.

During the Interregnum period plays were banned but they were re-established at the Restoration. The most famous other playwright of the period is probably Ben Jonson (1573-1637).

Discussion and activities

- Ask the children if they have heard of any of Shakespeare's plays.
- Working from the picture on page 35, get the children to make a model of the Globe. **Te**
- Make posters advertising a forthcoming play by Shakespeare at the Globe. **Ar**

36/37
Adventurers – Sir Francis Drake

Background information

Early life

Francis Drake was born on a farm near Tavistock in Devon. Drake became a sailor early in his life. When the master mariner whom he served died and left him his ship, Drake returned to Devon. Many famous sailors of the time including John Hawkins, lived in Devon. Drake joined Hawkins on a voyage to the West Indies to trade in slaves. Later he stole Spanish treasure and returned home a wealthy man.

Around the world

Drake's circumnavigation of the world began in 1577. He set off with five ships, his own being the *Golden Hind*. He sailed down the coast of Africa, called at the Cape Verde Islands and crossed the Atlantic. When they were off the coast of Argentina Drake had one of his captains, Doughty, executed for mutiny. Drake crossed the Magellan Straits and pillaged Spanish ships off the West coast. He went as far north as California where he landed. He now crossed to the Philippines and sailed around the Cape where a storm destroyed all the ships except the *Golden Hind*. He returned to England in 1580. He was given a hero's welcome by Queen Elizabeth despite Spanish protests. She knighted him.

Later life

Later Drake had a prominent role in the defeat of the Spanish Armada. His last voyage was with John Hawkins to the West Indies in 1595 when he died of fever.

Discussion and activities

- Do the children think that Drake was a hero or a pirate? What did the Spaniards think? **Hi 2**
- Trace Drake's route using a globe or atlas and the map on page 37 in the *Pupils' Book*. **Gg**
- Ask the children to put the information on the map on page 37 in the *Pupils' Book* into an illustrated diary as though Drake had kept it himself. **En 3**

38/39
Adventurers – Sir Walter Raleigh

Background information

Court favourite

Walter Raleigh was born into a prosperous family in Devon in 1554. His father had many friends in high places. When only 14 years old Raleigh fought for the French Protestants against the French King. He went on to Oxford University to study law. The Earl of Leicester introduced him to the Court in 1577. Elizabeth I and he seemed to get on well together. Against Elizabeth's wishes Raleigh married one of her ladies-in-waiting, Elizabeth Throckmorton. The Queen imprisoned them both for a short time.

Adventurer

Elizabeth gave Raleigh leave to found new colonies in the Americas. He sent two well-equipped expeditions. The colony of Virginia was formed, the first settlement was at Roanoke Island. It was as a result of these expeditions that potatoes and tobacco were introduced to England.

Later life

When James I became King he did not trust Elizabeth's favourites and had Raleigh imprisoned in the Tower of London. While there he was able to have books, to carry out scientific experiments and to receive visitors. He even taught Prince Henry, James' son, about astronomy. When Raleigh offered the King the chance to gain gold from the Americas he was released. James was trying to make peace with the Spaniards at the time so when Raleigh returned after attacking a Spanish fortress he was tried and executed in 1618.

Looking at evidence

Thomas Fuller in 1663 recalled the story of Elizabeth walking on Raleigh's cloak, which he had placed over a puddle.
'This Captain Ralegh coming out of Ireland to the English Court in good habit – his clothing being then a considerable part of his estate, found the Queen walking till, meeting a plashy place (*a puddle*), she seemed to scruple going thereon. Presently Ralegh cast and spread his new plush cloak on the ground; whereupon the Queen trod gently on it'.

Discussion and activities

- Ask the children to defend Raleigh's action by comparing it with Drake's. Do the children think that times had changed between Drake's exploits and Raleigh's? Ask them to explain why. **Hi 3/3**

40/41
Plague

Background information

Bubonic plague

The plague was a disease spread by germs carried on black rats. Black rats were the most common rat in the 17th century. In London they could live on the ships, in the narrow alleyways and could easily make holes in the walls of the houses. People who caught the plague often felt as if they had a chill, followed by shivering, a high fever, and a delirium. Then they would get the black blisters (buboes). If these burst there was a chance the victim might live, but a rash of red spots was a sure sign of death.

Cures

Strong-smelling substances such as vinegar, smoke and flames from a fire, the sweet scent of flowers (posies) were all tried. The authorities in London thought that shutting the house up would prevent the spread of the disease.

The Great Plague

The plague of 1665 killed about a quarter of all Londoners. We can not be sure exactly how many died from the plague because relatives tried to cover up the fact that someone in their family had contracted the disease.

The plague village

The plague hit other parts of England as well as London. The most famous outbreak is that in the village of Eyam in Derbyshire. A tailor contracted the plague from some cloth sent from London. It quickly spread and the vicar, Mr Mompesson, persuaded people to stay in the village instead of spreading it to nearby villages. 260 out of 350 people died.

Discussion and activities

- Set up a role play for the children of a plague infected family. How do they and their neighbours react?
- Tell children the nursery rhyme about the plague. Can they match the symptoms to the rhyme?
    'A ring, a ring of roses
    A pocketful of posies
    Atishoo, atishoo
    We all fall down'.
- Charles II and other rich people left London but the villagers of Eyam stayed in their village. Ask the children to explain these different points of view.
- Ask the children to explain how the plague managed to spread so easily and why it killed so many people. **Hi 1/3b**
- BLM 15 – Writing diary entries for a doctor at the time of the Plague. **En 3/2**

42/43
The Great Fire of London

Background information

Fire

Fire was particularly dangerous in towns. The houses were timber framed often with thatched roofs. Coal and wood fires were used for cooking and heating and candles were used for lighting, even in the streets. The narrow streets formed wind tunnels and so the fire could spread easily.

The fire starts

During the night one of Thomas Farynor's maids discovered that one of his baking ovens was alight and that the house had caught fire. Farynor could not put it out and his family jumped from the window to safety. The fire spread to the stables of the Star Inn and from there caught rapid hold. We know that Pepys' maid, Jane, woke him at three o'clock in the morning to tell him of the fire.

Fighting the fire

Fires were usually put out with water using buckets and a stirrup pump (pictured on page 42) but because 1666 had been a dry year there was not enough water to put out the fire in this way. Another common tactic was to pull the burning thatch off the roofs but the Fire of London had too good a hold. The drastic solution was to make a fire break by pulling down houses, or even blowing them up. The Lord Mayor tried to get Londoners to do that but most were too busy trying to escape. Pepys met the Lord Mayor in Canning Street and he said,
"Lord, what can I do? I am spent. People will not obey me. I have been pulling down houses but the fire overtakes us faster than we can do it."

By the time the King lent his authority to fighting the fire it was really too late. Only a change in the wind eventually put the fire out.

Destruction

London was never the same after the four days of fire, 86 churches and 13,000 houses (80% of all the houses) in the city were destroyed. Many people were homeless and the streets were awash with burnt remains, water and rubbish. Charles II took control. He had tents erected for the homeless and had the rubbish cleared.

Rebuilding

John Evelyn and Christopher Wren suggested new street plans but this could not be afforded. New stone or brick houses were built according to the old layout. Only a few streets were widened. Wren was employed to rebuild 51 churches, the most famous of which is St Paul's Cathedral.

Discussion and activities

- Ask the children to compare the syringe on pages 42 with pictures of modern day equipment. Drawings of old and new equipment and explanation of their use should be made. **Hi 1/2c, 3a**
- Ask the children what they might have done if they had been a Londoner at the time. Make sure they can use the evidence from pages 42/43 to justify their answers. **Hi 3/3**
- Using various red and orange papers as a back drop, make a picture of the fire using black as the shapes of the silhouetted buildings. Children's writing about the fire can be mounted amongst the flames. **Hi 1/4c**
- Ask the children to use either a computer programme like Front Page Xtra to make a newspaper, or a tape recorder to make a radio report of the fire. **En 3; Te 5/3a**
- Discuss with children the dangers of fire. **Sc 3/2b**
- BLM 16 – Writing a newspaper report of the Great Fire. **En 3/2b**

Science

Background information

Scientific revolution

Literature and the arts flourished in Tudor England as the full effect of the ideas based on Ancient Greek and Roman writings spread across Europe. In Tudor times the Ancient historians were especially popular and many English translations were made of their work. It was during the Stuart period that England entered the scientific revolution. There was a remarkable change in thinking whose hallmark was the application of experiment and reason to gain an understanding of the world. At the forefront of this revolution were William Harvey and Isaac Newton.

Harvey

Before Harvey's time people knew that the heart was important but did not know how it worked or what it did. Nobody before Harvey realised that all the blood came back from the veins into the heart and then around again.

Newton

The most important of Tudor and Stuart scientitsts was Isaac Newton (1643-1727). He worked out how the earth and other planets would be likely to move around the sun, and the moon around the earth, if they were all pulling on one another with the same force, gravity.

Newton was aware that his generation were only just beginning to scrape at the surface of scientific knowledge.

Navigation

This was a period when ships were beginning to sail away from coasts across oceans. Better ways of finding out the location of a ship were discovered.

PUPILS' BOOK NOTES 17

The best way was still by taking sightings from the sun and stars but new instruments were made: astrolabes and quadrants. Accurate clocks (chronometers) were also made so that ships could know for how long they had sailed in a particular direction. Using time and sightings the captain could work out the ship's longitude.

Astronomy

These new instruments and the ability to make powerful telescopes enabled closer study of the stars and of the moon.

The Royal Society

Charles II was very interested in all the new ideas and soon after his Restoration he founded the Royal Society to enable scientists to share and criticise each other's ideas. Anyone could attend the meetings of the Society, though Pepys found it all rather above his head.

Discussion and activities

- Ask the children to answer these questions:
  - How does blood get around the body?
  - Why does an apple hit the ground when it falls from a tree?
  - What does the surface of the moon look like?
  - What microscopic thing gives us colds?

  Then ask them if a Tudor child would have known the answers to those questions.

  Hi 1/3a; Sc 4/3c

- Use page 8 in the *Exploration and Encounters Teachers' Handbook* to explain more about navigation in the period.
- Identify lines of longitude on an atlas.
- Encourage the children to point to the approximate positions of the major organs of the body, or draw a diagram to show them. **Sc 2/4a**
- Make diagrams and descriptions to show the changing shape of the moon over a month. **Sc 4/3e**

46/47

Religion and superstition

Background information

The Authorised Version

Many people could not read and few could afford a Bible to have at home. The Bible was not such a common household book in Tudor and Stuart times as it is today. For most people their acquaintance with the Bible was through the church. There would be one copy in the church from which the clergy would read to the congregation. People had to learn it by heart if they wanted to think about it later.

James I was determined to help unify the church. Early in his reign he called the Hampton Court Conference of bishops and other learned men. At this conference it was agreed that an up-to-date English version of the Bible was needed so that everybody could use the same Bible. The result was what we call the King James Authorised Version that is still popular today.

During the Stuart period other religious books and pamphlets were produced. The most famous is John Bunyan's *Pilgrim's Progress*. This was about the difficulties and dangers Christians meet during their lives.

Witches

People are often uncomfortable about other people who live differently. One group who came under suspicion in the 16th and 17th centuries was the old widow or spinster. She would seem suspicious because she lived alone. She might even have a cat for company or to catch mice, but cats were also regarded as slightly magical. She almost certainly gathered herbs from the hedgerows; and this could be interpreted as gathering ingredients for magical potions. Most people did these things, but when a scapegoat was required for a poor harvest or an illness people found it very easy to blame those who lived alone in a different way from the majority.

Persecution

A number of people were persecuted throughout the period, usually for their religious beliefs – sometimes for being a Protestant, sometimes for being a Roman Catholic, or for being a Puritan, or for not being puritanical enough. Often these people became like modern day refugees, fleeing from one country to another. In 1620 some Puritans left Europe altogether, sailed from Plymouth, and established a colony in America called New Plymouth. In 1621 they gave thanks for their first harvest and the survival of their settlement. That event is still remembered as Thanksgiving Day in the USA.

Discussion and activities

- Do the children think its fair that some people are picked on just because they are different? Can they think of modern examples? **Hi 2**
- Make a display of various translations of the Bible. Ask the children to compare a favourite bit of them. **Re**
- Some people are still superstitious today. Can the children make a list or illustrated chart to show some common examples. (e.g. not walking under ladders, throwing salt over a shoulder, etc.).

Key *Tudor and Stuart* events

Date	Event
1455-1485	The Wars of the Roses. The House of York and the House of Lancaster fight over the crown of England.
1485	Henry Tudor (of the House of Lancaster) defeats Richard III (of the House of York) at the Battle of Bosworth Field.
1485-1509	Henry VII reigns.
1509-1547	Henry VIII reigns.
1534	The Act of Supremacy is passed by Parliament, making Henry VIII Head of the Church of England.
1536-9	The Dissolution of the Monasteries.
1545	The *Mary Rose* sets sail from Portsmouth to fight the French navy, but sinks and 600 men drown.
1547-1553	Edward VI reigns.
1553-1558	Mary I reigns.
1558-1603	Elizabeth I reigns.
1564-1616	William Shakespeare.
1577-80	Drake circumnavigates the World.
1587	Mary Queen of Scots is executed.
1588	The English navy defeats the Spanish Armada at the Battle of Gravelines.
1603-1625	James I reigns. The crowns of Scotland and England are joined.
1605	The Gunpowder Plot. Guy Fawkes and other Catholic plotters attempt to blow up James I and the Houses of Parliament.
1611	The King James Bible is printed.
1620	The *Mayflower* sails to America.
1625-1649	Charles I reigns.
1628	Dr William Harvey proves that the heart pumps blood around the body.
1642-1648	Civil Wars.
1649	Charles I is executed.
1649-1658	Oliver Cromwell rules.
1660	The monarchy is restored, and Charles II reigns.
1665	The plague hits London, killing nearly 70,000. It continues to spread throughout the country until March 1666.
1666	The Fire of London destroys 80% of the city's buildings in four days.
1685-1688	James II reigns.
1689-1702	William III and Mary reign, but the power to rule the country is now held by Parliament.

Further references

Books for teachers

- English Heritage, *Food and Cooking in the Sixteenth and Seventeenth centuries*, 1985.
- T. Kelly, *Children in Tudor England*, Stanley Thornes, 1987.
- J. Nichol, *Evidence in History: The Tudors*, Basil Blackwell, 1982.
- J. Nichol, *Evidence in History: The Stuarts*, Basil Blackwell, 1982.
- J. Ruby, *Costume in Context: Tudors and Stuarts*, Batsford, 1987.

Books for children

- R. Burrell, *The Tudors and Stuarts*, Oxford University Press, 1980.
- S. Butters, *Tudors Seafarers*, Oxford University Press, 1989.
- M. Connatty, *The National Trust Book of the Armada*, Kingfisher Books, 1987.
- A. Clarke, *Growing up in Elizabethan Times*, Batsford, 1980.
- E. Cooper, *The Mary Rose*, Macmillan, 1984.
- E. Harper, *Sir Francis Drake*, Ladybird Books, 1977.
- M. Jones, *Growing up in Stuart Times*, Batsford, 1979.
- J. Jessop, *Tudor Towns*, Wayland, 1990.
- G. Middleton, *Tudors, Stuarts and Georgians*, Longman, 1981.
- T. Pashley, *Living History: The Tudors*, Wayland, 1985.
- T. Triggs, *History in Evidence: Tudor Britain*, Wayland Publishers Ltd, 1989.
- D. Turner, *King Henry VIII*, Wayland, 1987.
- D. Turner, *Queen Elizabeth I*, Wayland, 1987.
- A. Steel, *The Stuarts*, Wayland, 1986.
- B. and A. Steel, *Cavaliers and Roundheads*, Wayland, 1986.
- R. Unstead, *Life in the Elizabethan Court*, A. and C. Black, 1974.

Fiction

- P. Lively, *The Ghost of Thomas Kempe*, Piccolo.
- D. Rees, *The House that Moved*, Young Puffin.
- G. Trease, *Cue for Treason*, Puffin.
- A. Utley, *A Traveller in Time*, Puffin.

Television

- *History 5-11: Tudors and Stuarts*, BBC, 1991-2. Five programmes of which two cassettes can be bought from the BBC School Radio and Cassette Service, Broadcasting House, London, W1A 1AA. Teachers' guides are also available for each century.
- *Timelines: Tudors and Stuarts*, Granada TV, Spring 1992. Five programmes and two computer resource units available from Mercury Education Productions, 8-10 Lower James Street, London, W1R 3PL.

Places of interest

The following museums have Tudor or Stuart collections:

- The Cromwell Museum, Grammar School Walk, Huntingdon, Cambs. This museum is devoted to Oliver Cromwell, containing family portraits, personal belongings, and objects to place him in his historical context.
- Hampton Court Palace, Richmond, London. Built by Cardinal Wolsey, this palace contains evidence of Tudor decor, Wren's baroque architecture, the Great Hall commissioned by Henry VIII, and vast Tudor kitchens.
- Hever Castle, Hever, Nr Tonbridge, Kent. Anne Boleyn's birthplace.
- Knole House, Sevenoaks, Kent. A Jacobean house, begun in 1456 and extended in 1603 by Thomas Sackville, to whom it was granted by Elizabeth I.
- Linlithgow Castle, Linlithgow, West Lothian, Scotland. The birthplace of Mary Queen of Scots.
- The Mary Rose Museum, H.M. Naval Base, Portsmouth. The collection comprises a large section of the hull of the ship, and 19,000 finds from the wreck site. For children's 'hands-on' experience of the Tudor gunnery, apply to The Mary Rose Trust, College Road, H.M. Naval base, Portsmouth, PO1 3LX.
- The museum of London, London Wall, London. The Great Fire, and Plague displays.
- The National Maritime Museum, Greenwich, London, SE10 9NF.
- The National Portrait Gallery, St Martin's Place, London, WC2H 0HE.
- The Old House, High Town, Hereford. A fine example of Jacobean domestic architecture.
- Shakespeare Globe Museum, Bear Gardens, Bankside, London SE1 9EB.
- The Shakespeare Centre, Henley Street, Stratford-upon-Avon, Warwickshire. The trust administers five Shakespearean properties, which include Shakespeare's birthplace and Anne Hathaway's cottage. The collections include Shakespearean memorabilia, Tudor and Jacobean furniture and furnishings.
- St Paul's Cathedral, London. The greatest of the 51 churches built by Wren after the Fire of London.
- Tower of London. The prison for many eminent Tudor and Stuart people. The museum now contains the royal armouries.

Read-aloud stories

The Royal prisoner
Charles I at Carisbrooke Castle

My name is Henry Firebrace. I was a young man at the beginning of the Civil Wars. Like many people in England, I did not know whether to support the King or Parliament. In the end I decided to support Parliament. I was sent to serve at Carisbrooke, a really old castle on a lovely island.

As I rode up to the castle, on a fine summer's day, I could see what a beautiful place Carisbrooke was. But I was soon to find out that Carisbrooke was also a very dangerous place, a place where I would have the greatest adventure of my life. For Carisbrooke Castle had a very special prisoner – the King!

The Civil War had been terrible. Many battles had been fought and many people killed. King Charles I had been captured by Parliament, but he had escaped and fled to Carisbrooke Castle. The young Governor of the island was called Colonel Hammond. The King tried to persuade Hammond to help him fight against his enemies. But the young Governor refused. He also refused to let Charles leave the island. The King was a prisoner!

Now when you hear me say 'prisoner' you probably think of a man held in chains in a dark cell. But Charles wasn't that kind of prisoner. He was still the King. Colonel Hammond did everything he could to make King Charles comfortable. He lived in a suite of royal rooms in the old castle, attended by his own servants. Luxurious carpets, curtains and tapestries for the walls were brought from Hampton Court Palace, and lavish meals were served. Charles was allowed to ride his horse round the island, and to go hawking and hunting. He had visits from the nobility of the island as well as two of his younger children, Princess Elizabeth and Prince Henry. At Christmas time, the King took rides in his royal coach, brought specially from the mainland. Colonel Hammond had a bowling green and summerhouse made for the King. And he encouraged His Majesty to walk along the battlements for exercise. This was certainly a better life than imprisonment in Hampton Court Palace, where the King had been before.

I knew that Colonel Hammond felt some loyalty towards Charles. Hammond once said, "I resolved it my duty to the King, Parliament and the kingdom, to use the utmost of my endeavours to preserve his person." I think the Colonel wanted to keep the King safe at Carisbrooke, and to stop any supporters of Parliament from harming the King.

I also found it difficult, keeping a King prisoner. At the back of my mind I kept thinking, "God made Charles my King. I am the King's subject. I should obey his every command." I also heard about the things Oliver Cromwell's New Model Army were doing. They had pushed Parliament aside and were now ruling the country. It seemed to me that the country would be better off if the King was back on the throne. And so I decided to change sides and help Charles. But things soon took a turn for the worse at Carisbrooke.

Colonel Hammond discovered that Charles had been secretly writing letters to his wife, Henrietta Maria in France. The King was telling his wife of his secret plottings with the Scots to invade England. Charles was writing other secret letters plotting to escape from the castle. He planned to break out of his cell and take a ship from the island to Southampton and then on to France. Hammond arrested the captain of the ship which was to rescue Charles. The captain was later tried and executed for trying to help Charles to escape. All these events made Colonel Hammond put guards on patrol along the walls and to lock the King in his bedroom at night.

I determined to plan a more secret and successful escape. It was to happen on March 20th, in the year 1648.

I was in the perfect position to help. As Page of the Bedchamber to King Charles, I was allowed to do guard duty outside the King's bedroom in the main building of the castle. Colonel Hammond had no idea that I was now a Royalist. I prepared the way by bribing the maids to take notes to the King when they brought back the laundry. They left the notes under the carpet in a certain place that the King knew. And I whispered my plans to the King himself through a little hole in the wall, hidden under a piece of tapestry.

My plan was for the King to squeeze through the bars of his window, sit on a stick fastened across a piece of rope, and use the rope to swing down into the courtyard. The rope was hidden in the linen taken into his room by the maid. I promised to meet him in the courtyard and then to lower him over the castle wall. After this he would have to climb down a steep bank, over another bank, and then manage several ditches down to the very bottom ground. Two friends of mine were to be waiting outside the castle with horses to take him to the coast, where a ship would take him to France.

I gave the maid a letter, signed 'David Griffin', in which I warned him that he should test the window out beforehand, as it might be too narrow. But on the night of the escape the King did not pass the test. He got stuck in the window. He gave a loud groan, and only just managed to get back into his room. I was heartbroken. I hurried to the wall to warn my friends to go away, to avoid being caught. I realised that the next escape plan must succeed, otherwise the King, and probably I too, would be doomed.

Colonel Hammond had become even more suspicious, and moved the King to safer quarters – a room on the north side of the castle. At first I thought my second plan would be more difficult, because the room was much higher up. But I soon realised that it would actually be easier, because there was no courtyard to cross. My plan this time was for the King to loosen the iron bars of his new window with files and nitric acid. I sent to London for these.

I also had to bribe the three guards who stood on a platform outside the King's window. I gave them £100 each – a huge amount – to walk away as the King climbed out of the window. The King would then swing down the north wall on a rope and meet the same friends of mine outside. Everything was set up for March 28, just over one week since the last attempt.

But when Colonel Hammond went to the King's room and said, "I am come to take leave of Your Majesty, as I hear you are going away!", we knew we had been fiendishly betrayed. Two of the guards had told Colonel Hammond about the plan; and would you believe it, those vagabonds kept the money too! It hurts me even now to tell the tale.

The Colonel suspected that I had had something to do with the escape plan, and immediately dismissed me. I was in despair, and wondered whether I would escape with my life. But nothing worse happened. Probably the guards who wanted to keep their £200 kept their mouths shut about my part in the plot, so there were no grounds for actually arresting me. But it was bad enough for me to have failed my King.

My last news of His Majesty was that he was taken as a prisoner to Newport, in the centre of the island, on September 6th; then to Hurst Castle just across on the mainland. Later, I heard the terrible news that he had been executed outside his own Whitehall Palace, on January 30th, 1649. He is the only monarch of our country to have been tried and executed by his own people.

When Charles II became King of England I told him, through my tears, how my failure to help his father had led to the King's execution in 1649. Although the kind-hearted King has rewarded my loyalty by making me a Clerk of the Royal Kitchen, his father's sad face at Carisbrooke will always haunt my dreams.

(In 1685, the last year of Charles II's life, Henry Firebrace was knighted by the King, and became Sir Henry Firebrace.)

An Elizabethan merchant
(The story of Robert Brerewood, 1532-1601)

This is the story of my father, Robert Brerewood, who lived in the city of Chester in Elizabethan England.

My father grew up in a village just outside Chester. My grandfather was a glovemaker, and my father learned how to make leather gloves by helping his father.

When Father got married, he moved into the centre of Chester. He set up his glove shop in one of a group of streets called The Rows. I remember running through those long, covered streets. They were very dirty and smelly. The buildings were three storeys high and made of wood. Father displayed all his gloves and leather in an open window. We all lived above the shop: Mother, Father, my two brothers, and me.

Father was a member of the Chester guild of glovemakers. Guilds were formed to protect the rights of their members, and to make rules about how goods should be sold. There were other guilds of shoemakers, wheelwrights, tailors, and many other trades in Chester.

When Father began to make more money, he built us a fine house in Bridge Street, near one of the town gates. Most of the other glovemakers, or glovers, also lived in Bridge Street with their families.

We had an apprentice living with us called William. William lived with us for eight years to learn glovemaking. This meant that Father had a helper that he didn't have to pay, while William lived and ate free of charge. We had great fun together. Sometimes we boys even joined William in the fights between rival apprentices.

Father began to think about other ways of making money. His glove business was going so well that he had the money to spend on starting another business. So he began to buy wool from sheep raised in Ireland. He sold the wool at a higher price to wool merchants in other parts of England. He also sold wood to Welshmen for building houses. Father even decided to do some farming. He was terribly busy, always rushing between his farm, his glove workshop, the ports where he bought wool, and the markets where he sold it. But he was becoming the most wealthy glover in Chester – almost as rich as the glovers in London.

Father was not only rich, he was also very popular. The people of Chester chose him as their mayor three times. As Mayor, Father looked after all the guilds, buildings and streets of Chester.

One Christmas Eve after he had become mayor, Father had to make a speech. But, like many other people, he could not read or write. So he told me what he wanted to say to the people. I had learned how to write at school, so I wrote his thoughts down. Then I read them out to him, over and over again, so that he learned his speech by heart. I was terribly proud of him when he gave his speech from memory!

Perhaps one of the reasons Father was popular was that he let the people of Chester enjoy themselves. Other mayors had tried to keep Chester a quiet and orderly place. But Father gave the people a three-day holiday at Whitsuntide. During these three days, the guilds, or all the craftspeople, got together and put on a big play for the town to watch.

Since I was part of the glovers guild that Father belonged to, I got to take part in the play. It was such fun! The guilds took stories from the Bible, and each guild acted out different parts of the story. Each company had a horse-drawn wagon. The upper part was a stage. In the lower part, we actors changed and made up for the plays. Throughout the three-day holiday, the wagons would form a procession throughout the streets of Chester, so that all the people could see the play. Those three days were some of the liveliest, noisiest and most exciting of the whole year!

At other times of the year, we enjoyed cock-fighting and bear-baiting. We played bowls in the narrow streets, and danced round the maypole. We also played at archery, football and cards.

Father was such a good mayor that he also became sheriff of the county of Cheshire. This was a very important job, for he had to carry out the orders of Queen Elizabeth herself!

Father and Mother became a 'gentleman' and a 'lady'. Because of their wealth and high position in society, they were allowed to wear bright colours, such as red and purple, that other people couldn't wear. They also wore furs, silks, velvets, and belts set with precious stones. I remember how grand they looked when they went for walks through the city!

Our last house was very big and expensive. It had thirteen rooms with large windows. We even had a framed portrait of Queen Elizabeth. Father was so popular that many of Chester's citizens gave him money to help build this house.

Father died in 1601. He had started as a humble glover but had become a mayor of Chester and sheriff of Cheshire, known at the court of Queen Elizabeth.

The longest journey
(The escape of Charles II after the battle of Worcester, 3 September 1651)

(There are many ports and towns mentioned in this story, so it may be helpful to refer to a map as you read it.)

A very tall man with dark ringlets on his shoulders and dark skin sat on his horse on the battlefield after the Battle of Worcester, in 1651. It was the young Charles II. He was a man with many friends and many enemies.

His friends and supporters, the Royalists or Cavaliers, believed that he was the rightful King of England and Scotland. His enemies, the Roundheads, believed that England should have a new type of government, without kings and queens. They had executed his father, King Charles I. Now England was at war again.

The Battle of Worcester had finished, but the outcome was not good for the Royalists. Charles sat on the battlefield and thought hard. He knew that his enemies, the Roundheads, had put a price of £1,000 on his head. They wanted to capture him, and he would have to escape quickly. He was going to need all his strength, courage, and inventiveness. They would soon be hot in pursuit of him, and Charles would need to count on the help of his Royalist friends to escape to safety in France. He knew that if he got to France, the King of France would protect him.

Charles turned to his friends for advice. Everyone had a different plan. The first plan was for him to ride to Scotland and join his loyal subjects there. So he started north, and came to a house called White Ladies House. Here, Charles knew he had some loyal Catholic followers. One of them, Richard, agreed to go with Charles on his escape.

But Charles had begun to feel uneasy about the plan to go to Scotland. He wasn't sure if he could trust the Scots. He decided instead to go to a Welsh port to find a ship for France. But first, he would have to be disguised. It would not do for the Roundheads to recognise him! So Charles gave away all his grand royal clothes. He gave away his precious watch, his royal garter, and all his valuable jewellery. He even had to say goodbye to his favourite horse, since it, too, would be recognised by his enemies. Then Charles put on some cloth breeches, a greasy hat, a leather doublet with pewter buttons, and a green jacket. He cut his long black ringlets off. Now he looked just like a farm labourer! He even took a false name. What would his mother and father have thought of his appearance now!

Charles and his friend Richard started walking towards the River Severn. They did not ride their horses because it was safer to be on foot in Roundhead country. They trudged through a wood. Poor Charles was not used to walking long distances. His feet were soon sore from his ill-fitting shoes, and his clothes became drenched by rain. After a dreadful day, the two men staggered to the house of a farmer, and hid in his barn. But the farmer advised against crossing the River Severn because it was carefully guarded by Roundhead soldiers.

So the plan had to be changed again. Charles decided to try to get a ship from near Bristol to take him to France. Richard was not sure that they should go to Bristol. He said, "Let's return to White Ladies House where we know it is safe. I think there may be a huge tree in the wood where you can hide until danger has passed." Charles agreed, and they walked back to White Ladies House. There they met a soldier friend of Charles, named Carlis. Carlis had fought beside Charles in the recent battle.

Charles changed into dry clothes. Then he went outside, where he found a huge oak tree, just as Richard had said he would. It was thick and very bushy. He climbed into the branches with Carlis. They were given enough bread, cheese and beer for the day. Charles was worn out with walking and he put his head in his friend's lap to sleep.

Suddenly, he woke up to the sound of soldiers marching just below him. The soldiers were Roundheads, and they were scouring the wood looking for him. Charles was frozen with fear. He watched the soldiers through the leaves, shouting at each other. He was relieved when they finally left the wood, and the startled birds returned to the trees.

By night time, Charles and Carlis were very stiff and sore from hiding cramped in the tree all day. They returned to Richard's house. Charles hid in a secret room, which was probably under the floor or behind a panelled wall. This tiny hiding place had been built for Catholic priests in Tudor times. There was a bed and some food and drink. Charles felt that he would be safer and more comfortable in this tiny room than in the oak tree. And so he was.

But it was not safe to stay in one place for too long. Charles' friends were sending secret messages out to seek a ship to take him from Bristol. Meanwhile, Charles and Carlis rode their horses to a house owned by another loyal Catholic. How glad Charles was not to be walking in ill-fitting shoes, and how much he liked his new horse! But as soon as they arrived at their lodging, Charles had to hide in a secret room once again.

A new plan was formed. Charles would ride towards Bristol with a lady called Jane Lane, disguised as her servant. He dressed as a farmer's son in a grey country tweed suit, and he changed his name again. Charles and Jane set off on one horse. Jane sat behind Charles on a special type of saddle. Charles wore a stout leather belt for her to hold on to. They had friends and servants with them. But there were many problems. The journey was very slow because of the weight carried by one horse. And then they lost their way in Bristol. Luckily, they found a house just outside the city where they planned to await a ship for France. But they discovered that no ship would sail from Bristol to France for a whole month.

Charles formed a new plan and went with his friends to Lyme Regis. At Lyme Regis, the men had been promised a ship for France. But when they got there, Charles and Lord Wilmot waited and waited. No ship came. They were promised another ship if they went to Bridport. But there they waited again in vain. Charles was now very depressed. He had to ride back to Dorset.

Soon Lord Wilmot had the good news of another ship. The men prepared again to travel. They left Dorset on horseback. Lord Wilmot did not bother to disguise himself. He and Charles rode towards Salisbury. On the way, the two men visited the famous stone circle at Stonehenge. Charles decided on a game to cheer them up. "Let's count the old stones here and see whether we get the same number!" Charles suggested. They counted them several times, but they never agreed!

The end of the journey now seemed in sight, but Charles could not relax until he reached France. From Salisbury he and Lord Wilmot rode by country lanes to an inn at Brighton, which was near the ship's port.

The ship's captain and his sailors did not know who would be sailing with them on their journey, and they were suspicious. But they had been bribed to go ahead and sail. Charles and Lord Wilmot were afraid, but they had to trust their luck. They sat down in a cabin to wait for the tide to carry the ship out to sea.

On the evening of 15th October, 1651, the little ship sailed from Shoreham and crossed the Channel to France. Charles was full of many feelings. He wondered now if he might still be King of England in the years ahead. And he couldn't wait to see his mother, Henrietta Maria, who was living in Paris.

When the ship finally landed in Normandy, the tired friends made their way on horseback all the way to Paris. Charles and his mother were joyfully reunited.

And just in time! Two hours after Charles had sailed from Shoreham, Roundhead soldiers rode into the town looking for "a tall black man 6 feet 4 inches high . . ."

Blackline Masters

The Blackline Masters extend themes developed in the *Pupils' Book*. They also provide additional forms of evidence to examine. The BLMs therefore encourage children to go back and re-examine the *Pupils' Books*, practise their information book skills, and to read with a purpose.

On each sheet the key skill or concept that the BLM develops is marked at the top. A full explanation of these key skills, and how they can be used as an ideal aid to assessment and record-keeping, can be found in the Key Stage 2 *Teachers' Handbook*.

Symbols are given at the top of some BLMs:

 = scissors needed

 = glue needed

The table below indicates the following:

- Which Blackline Master relates to each *Tudor and Stuart times Pupils' Book* page.
- Which Blackline Master resources different historical perspectives (political/ economic, technological and scientific/ social/ religious/ cultural and aesthetic).
- Which Blackline Master resources aspects of the thematic supplementary study units. (Valuable time-saving charts showing how *Tudor and Stuart times* can be linked with the supplementary study units can be found in the Key Stage Two *Teachers' Handbook*.)

Perspective/theme	Pupils' book page																						
	2	4	6	8	10	12	14	16	18	20	22	24	26	28	30	32	34	36	38	40	42	44	46
Political					5	7	8	9 10		10													
Economic, technical and scientific																				15	16		
Social				2			8	10		10													
Religious			1			7																	
Cultural and aesthetic				4																			
Ships and seafarers					5 6																		
Food and farming														12									
Houses and places of worship			1																		16		
Writing and printing				3																			
Land transport														14									
Domestic life, families and childhood				2						11		13		12	14					15	16		

Cause and effect
Points of view

Tudor & Stuart times

What do you think was the most important reason why Henry VIII closed the monasteries?
Add your own reasons in the empty boxes.
Cut out the boxes and arrange them in order of priority.

The monks and nuns in the monasteries still obeyed the pope.	Henry was worried that the monks and nuns may plot against him.	The monasteries were badly run.
Henry needed the money.	Henry wanted to show he was the real head of the Church in England.	Henry wanted to reward his friends with gifts and land from the monasteries.
The monasteries were wealthy and had too many possessions.	Henry wanted to make some of the buildings Royal houses.	Many people thought the monks and nuns were lazy.

BLM 1

© Ginn and Company Ltd 1992. Copying permitted by purchasing school only. This material is not copyright free.

Tudor & Stuart times

Looking at evidence
Communicating information

Queen Elizabeth is coming to stay! Make a programme of events to amuse her during her visit.

DAY 1

DAY 2

Points of view
Looking at evidence

Tudor & Stuart times

Many painters have done portraits of the Queen but none has sufficiently shown her looks and charms. Therefore Her Majesty commands all manner of persons to stop doing portraits of her until a clever painter has finished one which all other painters can copy. Her Majesty in the mean-time forbids the showing of any portraits which are ugly, until they are improved.

Written in 1570 by Lord Cecil, adviser to the Queen.

Although she was already 64, she was very youthful in appearance, seeming no more than 20 years of age.

Written by Thomas Platter in 1599.

Her face oblong, fair, but wrinkled. Her eyes small, yet black and pleasant. Her nose is a little hooked, her hips narrow. Her hair is an auburn colour, but false.

Written in 1597 by Paul Hentzner, a German writer.

What does this evidence tell you about Queen Elizabeth I?
Is all the evidence reliable?
Why do you think people had different opinions about the Queen?

© Ginn and Company Ltd 1992. Copying permitted by purchasing school only. This material is not copyright free.

Tudor & Stuart times

**Communicating information
Looking at evidence**

Miniature portraits were popular during Elizabethan times.
They were often worn as lockets or pendants.

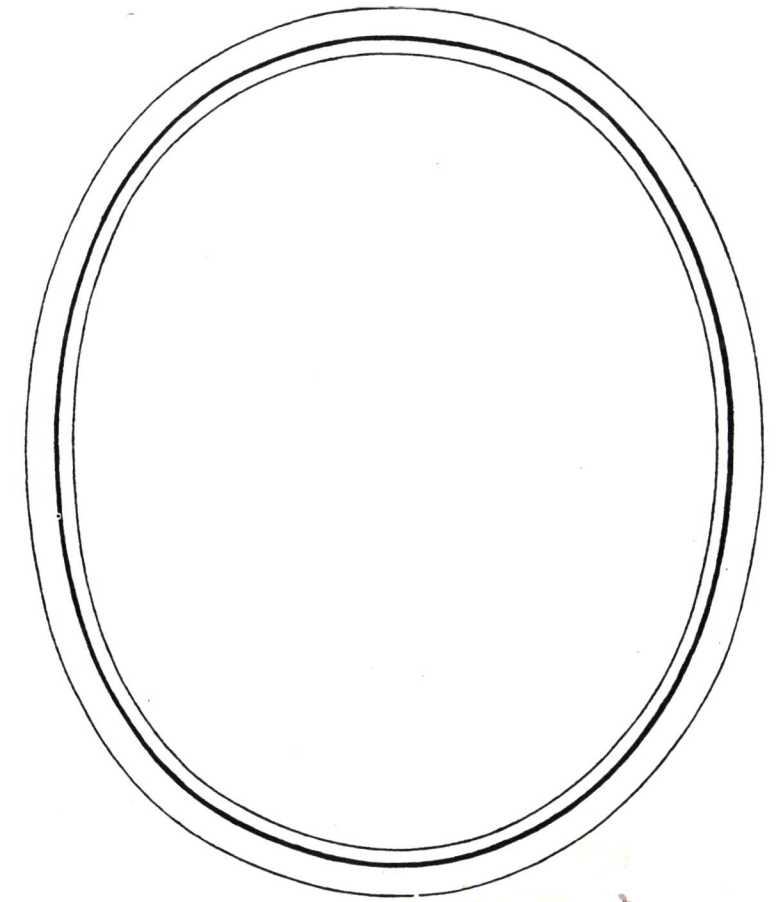

Make your own miniature of an Elizabethan person.

Chronology

Tudor & Stuart times

Cut out the pictures and arrange them in the correct order to tell the story of the Armada.
Add three of your own pictures to the sequence.
Write captions under the pictures to describe what is happening.

© Ginn and Company Ltd 1992. Copying permitted by purchasing school only. This material is not copyright free.

Tudor & Stuart times

Chronology

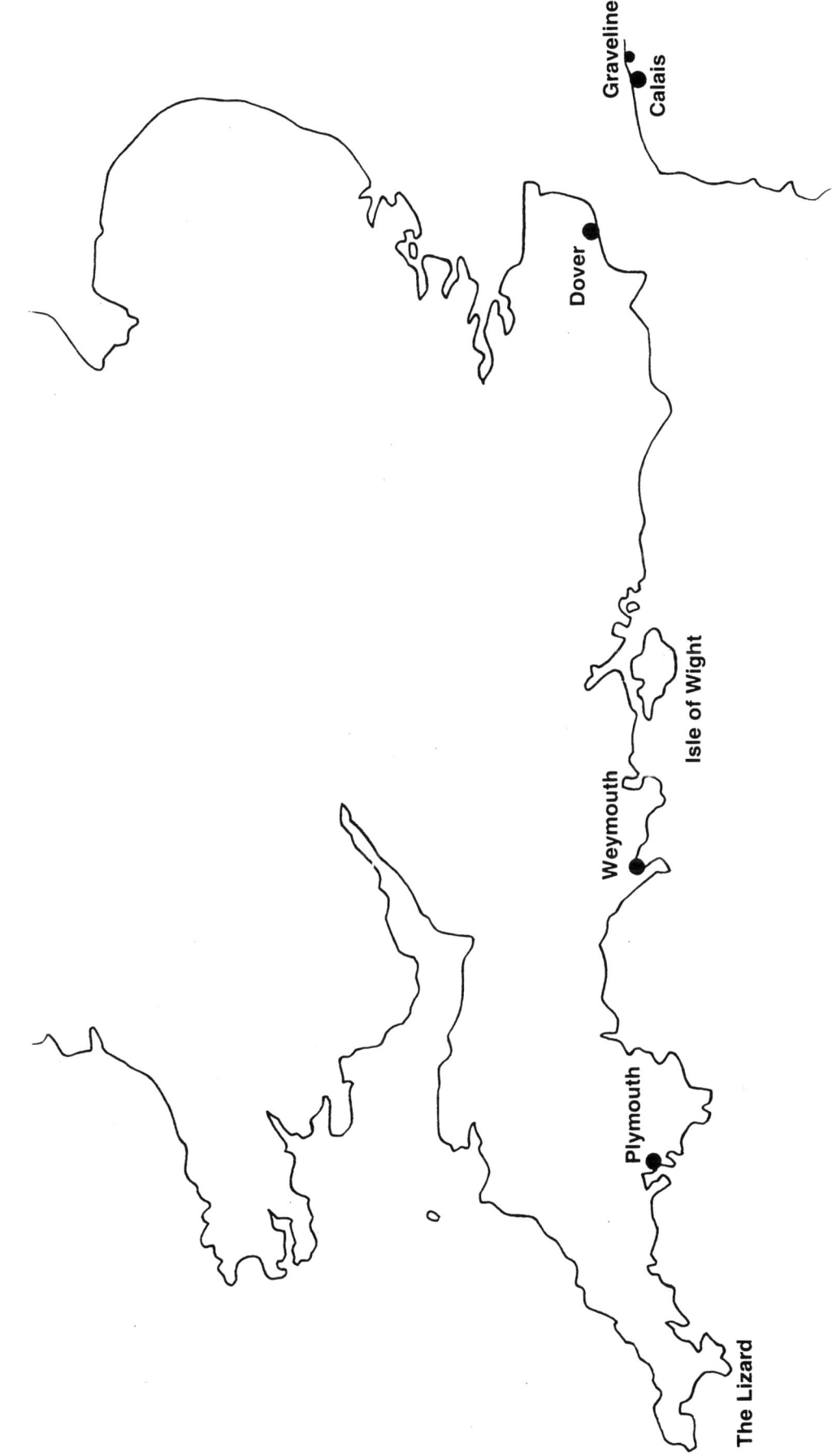

Mark the route of the Spanish Armada up the English Channel. It was sited off Land's End on July 29th, at Plymouth on July 31st, at Weymouth on August 2nd, at the Isle of Wight on August 4th and at Calais on August the 6th and 7th.

What message would you send from Plymouth to Queen Elizabeth in London on July 31st 1588?

**Cause and effect
Points of view**

Tudor & Stuart times

Pretend that you are Guy Fawkes writing a confession from the Tower of London before your execution.
Explain the reasons behind the plot and how the plot was organized.

Guido Fawkes

Tudor & Stuart times

**Points of view
Cause and effect**

1. Do you think it is right to fight against a king?
2. Who do you think should make the laws?
3. Who should decide what taxes you should pay?
4. Do you think a king should be able to arrest members of parliament?
5. Do you think the king should obey the laws of the land?

Pretend you are a Roundhead and a Cavalier.
Put your replies to these questions in the boxes beneath.

Roundhead　　　　　　　*Cavalier*

Make up your own questions and put the answers in the boxes.

© Ginn and Company Ltd 1992. Copying permitted by purchasing school only. This material is not copyright free.

BLM 8

**Points of view
Cause and effect**

Tudor & Stuart times

Death of a King

Imagine that you are a newspaper reporter.
Write a report of the execution of Charles I to send to soldiers in the New Model Army.
Ask a friend to write a report for cavaliers to read. Are the reports very different?

Tudor & Stuart times

Points of view

Charles II returned to England and was crowned king in 1660. What do you think the people in the crowd thought as he rode to his coronation?

| New model Army soldier | Royalist who had fought for Charles I | Owner of a theatre |

Looking at evidence

Tudor & Stuart times

> His majesty's attire was then an old sweaty leathern doublet with pewter buttons, a pair of old green breeches, and a jump coat (as the country calls it) of the same green, but so threadbare that it was worn white; a pair of his own stockings with the tops cut off because embroidered, and a pair of stirrup stockings which were lent him at Madeley; and a pair of old shoes cut and slashed to give ease to his feet, and an old gray greasy hat without a lining, a patched noggen shirt of the coarsest linen, his face and hands made of a reechy complexion by the help of walnut leaves. His handkerchief was very old coarse and torn, and daubed with blood as he suffered from nose bleeding.
>
> He had no gloves, but a long thorn stick, not very strong, but crooked three or four several ways in his hand. His hair cut short up to the ears.

Use this description to design a 'wanted' poster for Charles II.

Tudor & Stuart times   Communicating information

What goods are these shops selling?
Pretend that you are a Tudor shopkeeper.
Design your own shop sign to sell your goods.

Change and continuity
Communicating information

Tudor & Stuart times

In Tudor and Stuart times, when people died inventories were made of all their possessions.
These two inventories show the possessions of William Robinson and Richard Arnold.

Inventory of William Robinson, a farm worker. Died in 1600

His money and clothes	20 s
In the Living Room	
2 brass pots, 2 small pans, a cauldron	18 s
8 pewter dishes, 3 salt cellars, 3 candle sticks	7 s
A cupboard	6 s 8d
A table, a form, a plank, a chair 2 stools, a milk churn, 6 bowls, 2 barrels	2 s 8d
A poker, a spit, iron reckons attached to a gallow balke – (support for pots and pans)	2 s
In the Parlour	
2 cows and a heifer	£4 3 s 4d
A young pig	3 s
A cockerel and 2 hens	12d
In the Chamber (Upstairs)	
A bed, a wash tub and warming pan	3 s
A covering for a feather mattress	17 s
6 pillows and 5 blankets	
5 pillow cases, 2 napkins	6 s 8d
4 chests	5 s
Painted wall coverings in the house and chamber, ladders and all other wood in or about the house	
Total	£8 18 s 8d

Inventory of Richard Arnold a yeoman's son. Died in 1598

	s	d
Two jerkins	3	0
Two Dublets	10	0
One pair of hose and stockings	5	0
Two shirts	6	8
One hat	3	0
One pair of shoes	3	0
Summa (Total)	35	8

Match the pictures with the list of possessions on the inventories.
Make an inventory of the clothes you wear today.
Compare your inventory with that of Richard Arnold. Are there any similarities?

BLM 13

© Ginn and Company Ltd 1992. Copying permitted by purchasing school only. This material is not copyright free.

Tudor & Stuart times

Points of view

Why did these people need to travel on the roads?
What do you think they thought of the roads.

BLM 14

Points of view
Looking at evidence

Tudor & Stuart times

Imagine that you are a doctor living in London at the time of the plague.

June 1665

Write an entry for your diary for the day you visited your first patient who had the plague.
What were the patient's symptoms?

© Ginn and Company Ltd 1992. Copying permitted by purchasing school only. This material is not copyright free.

BLM 15A

Tudor & Stuart times

**Points of view
Looking at evidence**

September 12th 1665

Write another entry for September 1665.
More people are dying of the plague.
How might you try and cure them?
How do you protect yourself from the plague?

November 16th 1665

Write an entry for November 1665. What is it like to live in London now?
Compare your diary entries with those of a friend.

**Looking at evidence
Communicating information**

Tudor & Stuart times

London News

1st September 1666   Price 1d

Fire!

Imagine that you are a newspaper reporter at the scene of the fire of London. Describe what is happening.

Tudor & Stuart times

Chronology

Cut out the pictures and stick them in the correct order on a time line.

Change and continuity
Cause and effect

Tudor & Stuart times

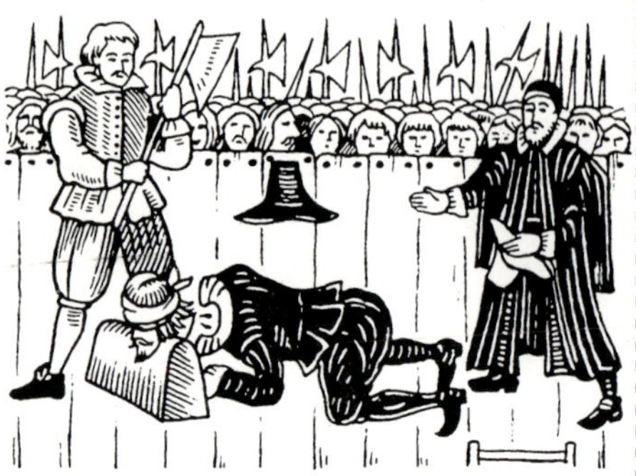

These pictures show people and aspects of life in Tudor and Stuart times. Cut out the pictures and arrange them according to whether you think they are features which belong to Tudor or Stuart times. Some features may belong to both Tudor and Stuart times.

© Ginn and Company Ltd 1992. Copying permitted by purchasing school only. This material is not copyright free.